WHISPERS FROM WITHIN

LINES THAT ILLUMINATE

RAGHAVENDRA KUMAR

Made with ♥ on the Notion Press Platform
www.notionpress.com

To my family, who have always supported my creative pursuits and encouraged me to follow my dreams.

To my friends, who have provided endless inspiration and laughter, and have been a constant source of love and encouragement.

And to all those who have touched my life in ways big and small, and have helped shape the person and writer I am today.

This book is dedicated to you, with deep gratitude and appreciation. May these poems bring you joy, comfort, and inspiration, and may they serve as a reminder that we are all connected by the shared experiences of the human heart.

Contents

Contents

Preface

Poetry is the art of turning our deepest emotions and experiences into a beautiful and meaningful form of expression. As a writer, I have always found solace and comfort in the world of poetry. It has been a cathartic process for me to pour my heart and soul onto the page, to share my innermost thoughts and feelings with the world. The poems in this collection are a reflection of my personal experiences, both good and bad. Each poem is a snapshot of a moment in time, a feeling or emotion that I have felt deeply and wanted to capture in words.

As I look back at the poems in this book, I am reminded of the many challenges and joys that I have experienced in my life. From heartbreak and loss to love and triumph, each poem tells a unique story of my journey through life.

I hope that these poems will speak to you in some way, that they will resonate with your own experiences and emotions. May they inspire you to embrace your own journey, to find beauty and meaning in both the highs and lows of life.

Thank you for taking the time to read this collection of poems. It is an honor to share these words with you, and I hope that they will bring you joy, comfort, and inspiration.

Prologue

Life is a journey that takes us through a myriad of experiences some joyous, some painful, and some that leave us forever changed. It is in these moments, both big and small, that we find the raw material for our creativity - the inspiration that fuels our art and gives it meaning.

In this collection of poems, I have drawn upon my own life experiences to explore the many facets of the human heart. From the simple pleasures of childhood to the complexities of love and loss, each poem reflects a moment in time, captured in words that evoke emotion, stir the soul, and illuminate the beauty of the human experience.

These poems are not just reflections of my own life, but of the lives of those around me - the people who have touched my heart and left an indelible mark on my soul. They are a tribute to the power of human connection, and to the resilience of the human spirit in the face of adversity.

As you read these poems, I invite you to come along on this journey with me, to feel the joy and pain of each moment, and to discover the beauty and meaning that lies within. For in these words, I hope you will find a reflection of your own life experience, and a reminder that we are all connected by the threads of our humanity.

1. Silent Echoes

In a world that values loud and outgoing,
Be true to your introverted self, don't doubt it.
Your thoughts and ideas, unique and profound,
Will take you places, if only you let them be found.

Don't shy away from the spotlight,
Stand tall and speak up, with all your might.
For the world needs your voice,
And your contribution, is just as important as any other choice.
Take time to recharge, in your own way,
But don't let fear hold you back from what you want to say.
For the world needs you, in all your quiet strength,
So embrace who you are, and go great lengths.
You are an introvert, and that is okay,
For the world needs both night and day.
So be yourself, and let your light shine,
For the world needs you, in your own unique design.

2. Rise and Shine

Rise like the sun,
Shine like a star,
Believe in yourself,
And go far.

Don't let the shadows,
Cast doubt in your mind,
For you have the power,
To be one of a kind.
With each step taken,
And each hurdle crossed,
You'll find the strength,
To break through the loss.
So don't be afraid,
To take the lead,
For you are the one,
With the power to succeed.
Embrace your uniqueness,
And let your spirit soar,
For the world needs you,
To be who you are.

3. Beyond the Horizon

Life is a canvas,
blank and bare,
But with every stroke,
you add color and flair.

Each day is a brush,
to paint with your dreams,
To build your own world,
and chase after its gleams.
So don't hold back,
or settle for less,
For in every small step,
you can find success.
Unlock your true potential,
with grit and with grace,
For you are the artist,
of your own life's canvas space.
With every brushstroke,
you will learn and grow,
As you create your masterpiece,
and let your unique colors show.

4. Man Unmasked

Being a man is not always easy,
For emotions run deep, and often uneasy.
We're told to be strong, to hide our pain,
To never show weakness, to never complain.

But the weight of the world, it can be heavy,
And the pressure to be perfect, it can be deadly.
We bottle up our feelings, deep inside,
And try to keep our emotions, firmly tied.
But the weight of our silence, it can be crushing,
And the mask we wear, it can be suffocating.
We long to be understood, to be seen,
But the fear of vulnerability, is often mean.
Being a man is not just about being tough,
But about being real, and speaking up.
It's about embracing our emotions,
And not being afraid, to show our devotion.
For being a man, is not just about strength,
But about being true to oneself, at any length.

5. Broken Promises

I thought love was supposed to be bright and true,
But with you, it's nothing but darkness and blue.
You brought out the worst in me, slowly but sure,
And I let you, because I thought love was pure.

You belittled me, made me feel small,
I gave up my voice, and let you have it all.
You played with my heart, and my mind,
I thought you were my everything, but you were just unkind.
I lost myself in you, forgot who I was,
But now I see, it's time to move on, because.
I deserve someone who treats me right,
I deserve love that's pure and bright.
I won't let you take any more from me,
I'm breaking free, from this toxic energy.

6. Intertwined Hearts

My love for you is like a rose,
Ever blooming and ever growing,
With each passing day it glows,
And my heart with it keeps glowing.

In your eyes, I see the stars,
That light up my darkest skies,
With you by my side, I go far,
And reach new heights of love and life.
Your touch ignites a fire,
That burns with passion and desire,
I'm forever yours, my one desire,
Together we'll conquer and never tire.
With every beat of my heart,
I know that we'll never part,
I'll love you now and forever,
My beautiful and precious treasure.

7. Shadows and Light

A soul once bright, now lost and alone,
In a world where darkness has grown.
Memories of light, now but a dream,
As the weight of life, burdens supreme.

A heart once full, now empty and cold,
As the passion of life, has grown old.
Dreams once alive, now fade away,
As the promise of tomorrow, turns to gray.
The path once clear, now shrouded in mist,
As the way forward, is no longer exist.
The road once straight, now winding and rough,
As the journey of life, has become tough.
But hope still lingers, in the depths of despair,
For a soul once lost, may still repair.
With strength and courage, and a will to survive,
The lost soul may yet, come back alive.

8. Embrace the Light

Life may be tough, and the road may be long,
But with a positive mindset, we can stay strong.
Through every storm, and every strife,
We can find the beauty, in the gift of life.

When the sun is shining, and the sky is blue,
With a grateful heart, we'll see all that's true.
The little things, that make our hearts sing,
Will help us remember, what truly living.
With every step, we take on our way,
We'll face the challenges, come what may.
With a positive attitude, and a smile on our face,
We'll find the strength, to win every race.
So let's embrace the journey, with open hearts and minds,
And let the positivity of life, be what we find.
For in every day, there is a chance to grow,
And in every challenge, there's a chance to know.

9. Dark Music

In the quiet of the night,
When the world is fast asleep,
A loneliness creeps in,
That cuts deep.

The emptiness echoes,
In the chambers of the heart,
A longing for connection,
A feeling that won't depart.
The mind races,
With thoughts of the past,
Of moments shared,
That didn't last.
The silence is deafening,
In the solitude of the soul,
A longing for company,
That makes one feel whole.
But even in the loneliness,
There is a glimmer of hope,
For in the darkness,
We learn to cope.
And as we learn to embrace,
The quiet of the night,
We find comfort,
In the loneliness of life.

10. Limitless

Distance stretches wide,
Between two hearts so true,
But love knows no bounds,
And will always find a way through.

Memories of the past,
And dreams of the future,
Keep the love alive,
And the heart's beat steady and pure.
Though miles may separate,
And time may pass so slow,
The bond between us,
Will forever grow.
With every call, every text,
Every letter in the mail,
The distance between us,
Will begin to pale.
For in the distance,
We find strength and trust,
And in the waiting,
Our love will only adjust.
So let us hold on,
To the love we share,
For distance may be great,
But it cannot compare.

11. Fly Like an Angle

The ocean stretches wide,
A canvas painted blue,
As I sit here alone,
My mind and heart feel renewed.

The waves crash against the shore,
A symphony of sound,
A reminder of the power,
That can be both fierce and profound.
The seagulls cry out,
In a language all their own,
As they soar above the water,
A sight that's never grown old.
The wind in my hair,
The sun on my face,
I take in the beauty,
Of this peaceful, quiet place.
Here in the stillness,
I find clarity,
In the midst of the chaos,
Of life's complexity.
So I'll sit here awhile longer,
In the company of the sea,
For the ocean has a way,
Of setting my soul free.

12. Dancing in Madness

In the rain they dance, with abandon and grace,
Their love on display, in a slow, intimate pace.
The drops fall around them, a symphony of sound,
As they sway to the rhythm, their feet barely touch the ground.

They hold each other close, in a tender embrace,
As if nothing else in the world exists in this space.
The rain is a curtain, shielding them from the world,
As they move in perfect harmony, their bodies swirl.
They laugh and they spin, under the open sky,
Their love is a beacon, burning bright and high.
The rain is a blessing, a gift from above,
A symbol of the love that they share, pure and true.
Their hearts are alive, with a passion that's real,
Their love like a fire, that nothing can steal.
In the rain they dance, in a moment of bliss,
Their love forever entwined, in a perfect kiss.

13. Last Portrait

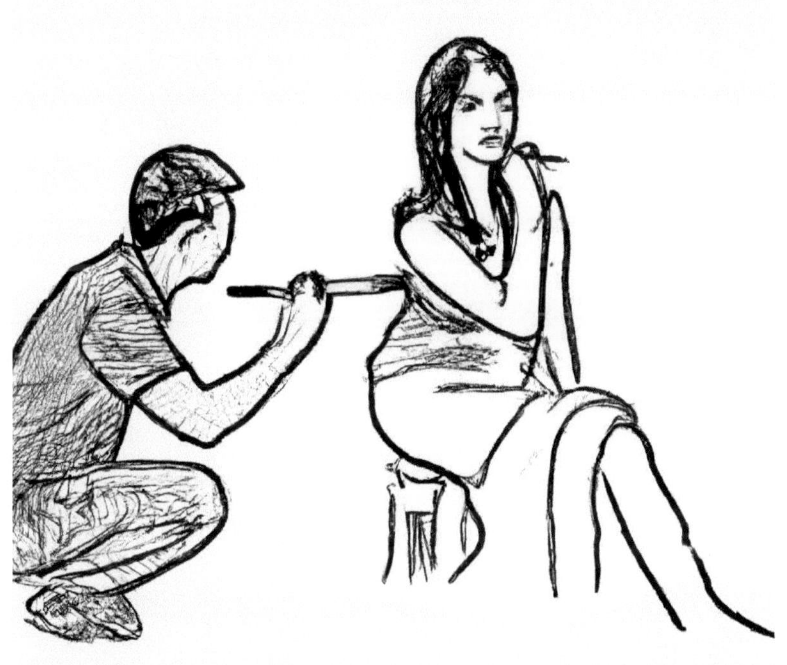

With brush in hand, and canvas on easel,
A boy sets out to paint a portrait of his belle,
He studies every line and curve,
Capturing the essence of her with every stroke, a nerve.

He paints her eyes, deep pools of brown,
That shine with love, and never a frown,
He paints her lips, full and red,
That whisper sweet nothings, as they lay in bed.
He paints her hair, a waterfall of black,
That cascades over her shoulders, in a gentle slack,
He paints her skin, soft and smooth,
That he longs to touch, and never to soothe.
He paints her smile, warm and bright,
That fills his heart with love, and never a blight,
He paints her spirit, free and wild,
That makes him feel alive, and never beguiled.
With every brushstroke, he pours his heart,
Into the painting, a work of art,
For she is his everything, his reason to live,
And in this portrait, she will forever give.

14. Song of Love

In your eyes, I saw the sun,
Shining bright, never done.
A light that guided me through dark,
And a love that left its mark.

In your touch, I felt the warmth,
Of a fire that never storms.
A comfort that soothed my soul,
And a love that made me whole.
In your voice, I heard the song,
Of a melody that never longed.
A harmony that filled my heart,
And a love that set us apart.
But now you're gone, and I'm alone,
With memories of you etched in stone.
Though you may be out of sight,
You're forever in my mind and heart, so bright.
This ode to you, my dear,
Is a token of love sincere.
For the memories we shared,
Will forever be ensnared.
In my heart, forever more,
You will be the one I adore,
The love of my past,
Will forever last.

15. Complexities and Nuances of Life

Life is a journey, a winding road,
Full of twists and turns, highs and lows.

It's a quest for meaning, a search for truth,
A puzzle to solve, in our quest for proof.
We ask ourselves, why are we here?
What is the purpose, what is the fear?
Is it to love, to learn, to grow,
To find happiness, before we go?
We strive for success, in our own way,
Chasing our dreams, day by day.
We seek fulfillment, in all we do,
Hoping to make a difference, in this world too.
But in the end, what does it all mean?
Will our lives have been lived, with purpose seen?
Perhaps it's not for us to know,
But to trust in something greater, and let it flow.
Life is a mystery, a work in progress,
Full of surprises, and tests of our mettle.
But if we live with love in our hearts,
And a spirit of gratitude, we will have done our part.
So let us cherish each day, and make the most,
Of the time we have, before we're called to the coast,
For the purpose of life, may be to live,
And leave behind, a positive give

16. Expression of Gratitude

The warmth of the sun on my face,
The gentle breeze in its embrace.
The sound of the birds in the trees,
Nature's symphony, a symphony of ease.

The taste of a fresh picked apple,
Juicy and sweet, so simple yet ample.
The smell of a home cooked meal,
Love and comfort, that's what it feels.
The sight of a loved one's smile,
A moment of joy, worth the while.
The touch of a hand on my heart,
A connection, that set us apart.
These simple pleasures, that we often miss,
Are the treasures, that make life bliss.
For in the midst of our busy days,
It's the small things that bring us grace.
So let us take a moment to pause,
And give thanks for the simple because,
For it's the ordinary moments, that make life grand,
And remind us to be grateful, for what we have in hand.

17. A Musing on the Passage of the Time and its Effects on the self

Time is a river, that flows ever on,
Carrying us with it, until we're gone.
It's a force that shapes us, day by day,
A constant reminder, that nothing stays.
As we journey through life, we can't help but see,
The effects of time, on you and me.
Wrinkles appear, and hair turns gray,
Reminding us, that time is here to stay.
We watch as the seasons, come and go,
A cycle that repeats, with each ebb and flow.
We watch as the flowers, bloom and fade,
A reminder, that all things, must eventually fade.
As we look back, on the path we've trod,
We see the moments, that have shaped us, and made us who we are.
We see the good times, and the bad,
But through it all, we've stood, and we've stood glad.
We can't stop time, in its endless race,
But we can choose how we spend it, in this place.
We can choose to live, with love in our hearts,
And leave behind, a legacy, that will never depart.
So let us embrace, the passing of time,
For it shapes us, and makes us shine.
Let us embrace the changes, and the growth,
For it makes us who we are, and all that we know.

18. A Reflection on the beauty and Fragility of Nature

Nature is a canvas, painted with care,
A masterpiece, beyond compare.

It's a symphony, of colors and hues,
A beauty that never chooses.
The mountains, majestic and grand,
Stand tall, with their snowy band.
The oceans, vast and deep,
Mysterious and full of secrets to keep.
The forests, lush and green,
A haven for all, to be seen.
The deserts, barren and dry,
A harsh landscape, that's a wonder, why.
Nature is a treasure, a precious gem,
A gift, that we should all esteem.
But its beauty is fragile, and fades with time,
A reminder, that we should all be kind.
We must take care, of the earth we tread,
For it's the only one, that we have, to be fed.
We must protect, its beauty and its grace,
For it's a treasure, that we can't replace.
Nature is a reflection, of our own souls,
A reminder, that we are all whole.
Let us cherish it, and let it be,
A reflection of our own humanity.

19. A Mind's Journey

My mind is a maze, a labyrinth of thought,
A place where my demons, are constantly fought.
A battle that rages, deep within my soul,
A war that's been fought, since I was young and whole.

My mind is a prison, a cage of fear,
A place where my worries, are always near.
A weight that I carry, day and night,
A burden that's heavy, a constant fight.
My mind is a canvas, a blank sheet of white,
A place where my creativity, takes flight.
A world of imagination, a realm of art,
A sanctuary, where I can play my part.
My mind is a journey, a path that's unique,
A place where my healing, takes its peak.
A process that's painful, but worth the cost,
A growth that's empowering, and never lost.
My mind is a part of me, a part of my being,
A place that's complex, and ever-seeing.
It's a place of struggles, and triumphs too,
A mind that's alive, and always new.
So I'll keep walking, this journey of mine,
With the knowledge, that I'll be just fine.
For my mind is my own, and I'll take the lead,
With the strength and courage, that I'll always need.

20. The Search for Self

I am a puzzle, a mystery untold,
With pieces that scatter, and stories untold.
A journey of discovery, a quest for truth,
To find my place in this world, and my youth.

I am a chameleon, ever-changing,
A shape-shifter, rearranging.
I try on different roles, different faces,
In search of my true self, in different spaces.
I am a mirror, reflecting the past,
A glimpse of my history, that never lasts.
Memories that shape me, experiences that mold,
A reflection of who I was, and who I'm told.
I am a canvas, a blank sheet of white,
A space to create, to explore and ignite.
I paint my own picture, with every brush stroke,
A self-portrait, that's unique, and evokes.
I am a work in progress, a never-ending story,
A search for my identity, my own glory.
I'll keep looking, and growing, and changing,
Until I find the answer, and self-arranging.
I am me, and that's all I'll ever be,
A unique individual, that's constantly free.
To be who I want, and to be true,
To myself and the world, that's what I'll do.

21. A letter to you

My dearest,

I sit down to write this letter to you,

With a heavy heart and a mind full of blue.

I know I messed up, and I caused you pain,

And for that, my love, I'm truly ashamed.
I know I can't change the past,
And the memories we shared will forever last.
But I want you to know, that I regret
The mistakes I made, and the love we forget.
I think of you often, and the times we shared,
The laughter and joy, and the love we dared.
I remember the way you smiled,
And the way you looked, when you were wild.
I wish I could turn back the clock,
And make things right, without any mock.
But I know that's not possible,
And the future is uncertain, and unstoppable.
I just want you to know, that I love you still,
And the thought of you, gives me a thrill.
I hope someday, you'll find it in your heart,
To forgive me, and we can make a new start.
Until then, my love, please know,
That you'll always be in my heart, and my soul.
Forever yours,
R……

22. Voyage

In search of myself, I wander far and wide,
Through valleys low and mountains high,
I seek the truth, that lies within,
The answers to the questions, that have always been.

I look at the world, through different eyes,
I listen to the stories, of truth and lies,
I try on different masks, to see which one fits,
But my true self, always seems to slip.
I explore the depths, of my own mind,
I unearth the secrets, I've left behind,
I challenge the beliefs, that once held me tight,
And in the process, I learn to shed the light.
I find my voice, in the silence of night,
I discover my strength, in the darkest of fight,
I find my purpose, in the things that I do,
And I realize, my identity is not just a skew.
It's a journey, that's never done,
A process, that's always begun,
To know oneself, is to know the world,
And the self-discovery, is a path, that's unfurled.
So I'll keep searching, I'll keep trying,
I'll keep climbing, I'll keep flying,
For in the end, it's not about the destination,
But the journey, that leads to self-realization.

23. The Light in the Darkness

In the darkest of times, when the shadows loom,
And the weight of the world, feels like it's in the room,
When the tears fall like rain, and the heart aches with pain,
It's easy to think, happiness will never be regained.

But in the midst of the storm, there's a glimmer of light,
A spark that still burns, in the long, dark night,
It's a reminder that hope, is never truly gone,
And that happiness, can still be found, even when all seems wrong.
For in the darkest of days, when the clouds are so low,
There's still beauty to be found, in the soft falling snow,
In the quiet of night, when the stars shine so bright,
There's still wonder to be found, in the world's pure light.
And even in the depths, of our deepest despair,
There's still a chance, for love and joy to repair,
So hold on tight, to that glimmer of hope,
And know that happiness, is just around the bend, it's scope.
For in the darkest of times, there's still a way,
To find the light, and chase the shadows away,
So hold on to hope, and keep on moving forward,
For in the end, happiness will be found, it's a reward.

24. The Beauty in the Struggle

The struggles we face, shape us like clay,
Molding us into the person we'll become one day,

With each blow, each twist, each turn,
We learn to stand tall, and our strength we earn.
Hardships come in many forms,
But through them all, we weather the storms,
We learn to be resilient, we learn to be brave,
We learn to find joy, in life's darkest cave.
For in the struggles, we find our true selves,
We discover our strength, and the power it delves,
We learn to appreciate, the little things in life,
The simple pleasures, that bring joy and light.
Through the struggles, we learn to let go,
Of what no longer serves us, and what we don't know,
We learn to find peace, in the present moment,
And to be thankful, for what we have, and what we've been given.
So let the struggles come, and let them shape you,
For in the end, they'll make you stronger, it's true,
And through them all, you'll find true happiness,
For it's in the struggles, we truly learn to appreciate and bless.

25. Betrayal

My heart was yours, my trust was true,
But you took it all, and left me blue,
With shattered pieces, and a mind full of doubt,
I'm left to pick up, what you knocked out.

I gave you everything, my love, my all,
But you trampled on it, and let it fall,
You played with my emotions, like a toy,
And left me to suffer, like a broken boy.
I trusted you, with my deepest fears,
But you used them, to bring me to tears,
You whispered sweet nothings, in my ear,
But they were all lies, that I couldn't hear.
I loved you, with all my heart,
But you tore it apart, and made it fall apart,
You said you loved me, but your actions said otherwise,
Leaving me with a broken heart and a soul in crisis.
But I won't be broken, I won't be destroyed,
For I'll rise from the ashes, and be overjoyed,
I'll learn from my mistakes, and move on,
For true love, is worth the struggle and the dawn.
I'll find happiness, and true love again,
And I'll make sure it's built on trust, not pretend,
For you may have broken my heart, but you didn't break my spirit,
I'll rise above it, and find a love that is truly merit.

26. Two Sides of Life

Happiness and pain, two sides of a coin,
One shines bright, the other, a constant join.
They may seem opposite, but they are not,
For one cannot exist without the other, in this life we've got.

Happiness brings joy, and laughter to the soul,
But pain reminds us, that life can be cruel,
It teaches us empathy, and how to grow,
And how to appreciate, the beauty that life bestow.
Pain can be a teacher, if we let it be,
It can show us, what we're made of, and what we can see,
It can help us find strength, and move on,
And to find a balance, that can be relied upon.
For in the balance, of happiness and pain,
We find understanding, and wisdom to gain,
We learn to appreciate, the good and the bad,
And to find peace, in the moments that we've had.
So let us embrace, both happiness and pain,
For they are both a part, of life's intricate chain,
For in the balance, we'll find a sense of peace,
And understanding, that will never cease.

27. Dance of Death and Life

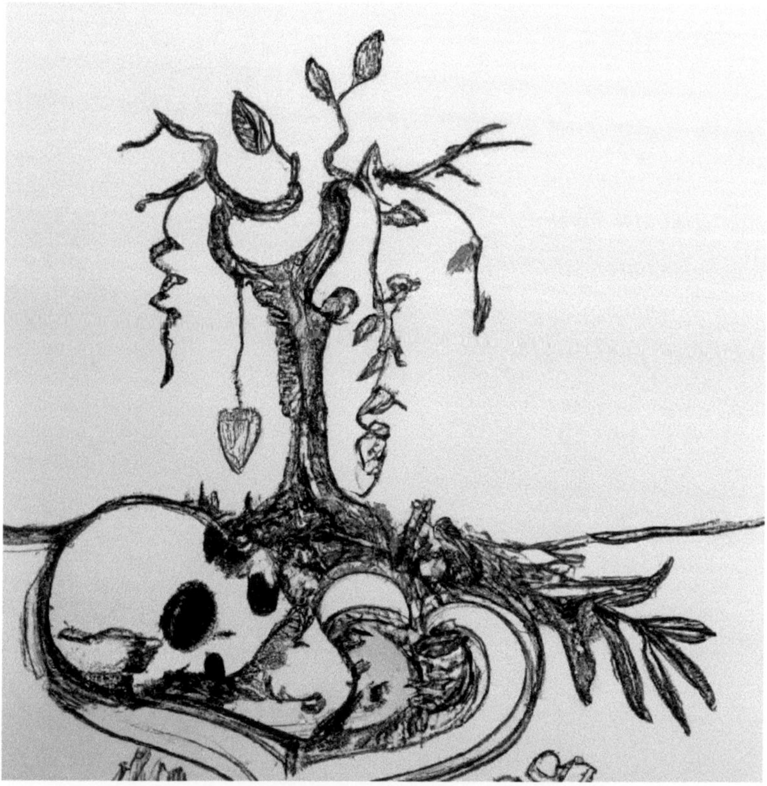

Death and life, side by side,
In a dance that never ends,
A constant cycle, unbroken ties,
A journey that never bends.

Death speaks of endings,
Of the final curtain call,
But life reminds us,
Of the beauty in it all.
Life speaks of beginnings,
Of hope and new days,
But death reminds us,
Of the preciousness of our ways.
Together they remind us,
Of the fleeting nature of time,
To cherish each moment,
And make the most of our climb.
So let us embrace,
Both death and life with grace,
For in their balance,
We find our place.

9 798889 866411

Printed by Libri Plureos GmbH in Hamburg,
Germany